Mr & Mrs Euge~~...~~   tl
    Really e
yáll.

MW00946668

[signature]
ARABA TEMPLE

THE FUNNY SIDE OF DEATH

A look at the funny side of death from the eyes of retired Funeral Home and Cemetery Owner, Lee B. Downs

by
Lee B. Downs with Dr. Kathleen B. Heath

authorHOUSE®

AuthorHouse™
1663 Liberty Drive, Suite 200
Bloomington, IN 47403
www.authorhouse.com
Phone: 1-800-839-8640

First published by AuthorHouse 7/31/2008

ISBN: 978-1-4389-0231-9 (sc)

Printed in the United States of America
Bloomington, Indiana

This book is printed on acid-free paper.

DEDICATION

To:

Harry C. Powell, President of the Lehigh Corporation; James G. Fortana, Senior Vice- President;

My wife, Frantastic Downs; Family- Sueann Downs, Terry Downs, Randy Downs, Tammi Sue Downs, Troy B. Downs, and grandson, little Lee Downs, all of my friends, and all the people who died or made preparations to die to make this book possible.

TABLE OF CONTENTS

GLOSSARY OF TERMS

BURIAL-	Final Disposition other than Cremation
CEMETERY-	Correct spelling for burial grounds. Cemetary- incorrect spelling.
CREMAINS-	Cremated Human Remains
CREMATION-	Final Disposition by Incineration
CRYPT-	Receptacle in a Mausoleum
ENTOMBMENT-	Burial in a Mausoleum
INTERNMENT-	Burial in the ground
INURNMENT-	Burial of an urn in a Niche
MAUSOLEUM-	A building or a Chapel of Crypts for Entombment
NICHE-	Receptacle for Urn and Cremated Remains

ABOUT THE AUTHOR

What kind of a guy goes into the funeral business? Just a regular guy like me. I was born in Birmingham, Alabama, but we moved to Florida when I was a baby. So, I tell everyone I am one of those rare birds- a real Floridian.

I joined the Navy after Korea when everyone wanted to go into the service. We had 146 of us from Miami join the Navy and Marine Corp., and we were sworn in at Tampa at the stadium and marched in the Gasparilla Parade in 1956. The Gasparilla Parade celebrates the heritage of pirates and buccaneers in Florida. Tampa's football team is called the Buccaneers and their stadium has old galleons. The day we marched, half of us were dressed as pirates and the other half as buccaneers.

Then they took us to the Great Lakes in January of 1956, the coldest month of the year. Most of us had never seen snow and only had short-sleeve shirts. After I got over being a young recruit, I spent almost twenty years as an Air Controlman and a Training Device Instructor. My last four years was as a recruiter in Southwest Florida with offices in Sebring, Arcadia, Labelle, and Fort Myers.

What kind of a guy gets into the funeral business? A guy that has seen a lot of death, firsthand. I was in a squadron in Rota, Spain during Viet Nam. I experienced my uncle's death. He had twenty-six years in the Navy. My father-in-law died. And I watched my executive officer and some of my shipmates crash and die. When I left Rota, I never dreamed I would end up in the funeral business.

But when I left there and was finishing my last hitch with the Navy as a recruiter, I started thinking about retirement. I got a part-time job with the Lehigh Corporation selling their cemetery properties door-to-door. I was selling insurance, too. My business card said, "We cover you from the womb to the tomb." They soon made me a sales manager and the president said if I could get sales to $15,000 a month, I could write my own paycheck. The first year we did $1,000,000 in pre-need (pre-arranged funerals) sales.

When I retired from the Navy, they promoted me to Vice-President of the Corporation in charge of Cemetery Operations. From there, I built a crematory. I went to many schools and seminars to learn the business. I bought a cemetery in Homosassa, Florida and then became part-owner of Anderson Funeral Home in Lehigh Acres, Florida.

I have been married to my wife, Frantastic for 17 years and was married to my ex-wife, Sue for 20. I have four children of my own. Fran has three. Between us, we have seven children, fifteen grandchildren, and five great-grandkids. We are now retired and travel in our motor home.

INTRODUCTION

"Good evening. I'm Lee Downs from Anderson Funeral Home." I could hear the T.V. blaring loudly from inside the house. "You called about pre-arranging your funeral?" Mrs. Smith, a silver-haired grandmother-type with granny glasses, grabbed me by the arm and pulled me in.

"I'm playing T.V. Bingo. You'll have to wait till the game's over to talk." She quickly sat down at the card table she had set up in front of the couch. I stood behind her and had a perfect view of her eight cards and the T.V. This was a bit unusual, but salesmen have to be ready for anything.

"N30."

"B4."

"O72."

How did she keep up? They were going so fast, and she had so many cards to mark.

"Hey, you missed one. O72 gives you Bingo on this card."

"Bingo?" She picked up the phone and called it in. When she hung up, I asked her about pre-arrangements.

"Give me the finest, damn casket and the best shady lot in the cemetery! When my number comes up, I want my friends to say 'she's still yelling Bingo from the grave!'"

Everyone's number comes up, eventually. Being in the business of burying people's loved ones and friends can be a very serious and stressful occupation. But I found out early on, in the 70's when I started my career in the bereavement business that it was important to keep my sense of humor to keep my sanity. My recollections from my encounters with the public, and from later owning my own cemetery and Funeral Home have prompted me to write this book. As pain-filled and hard as death can be, there is always a flip side to the coin. Sometimes, it is a lot healthier to laugh than to cry.

Laughing can release the inevitable tension that death and grieving create. Death is funny because people are funny. Humor is a very human characteristic. Animals, plants and trees don't have humor; only people. It is my hope that my life experiences in the death business provide laughter and healing, and open the reader's eyes to seeing "the funny side of death."

Sometimes, in my sales work, I ended up being the butt of the joke. One night, I had an appointment with a man whose wife wrote jokes for PLAYBOY Magazine. As always, when I enter someone's home, I admired their furnishings, décor and paintings. This couple had her Playboy jokes displayed all over the walls. I was there to discuss very serious business but I couldn't help laughing at the risqué jokes.

Then, they offered me a fancy Italian wine with a tongue twister of a name. I turned it down because I don't drink when I'm working. But they insisted, saying they would not do business with me unless I had a drink. I obliged, but anytime I mentioned the name of the wine they laughed at me. And I was still sober! Finally, they bought a complete pre-arrangement package, and I left a little embarrassed, but at least I had made a big sale.

In fact, I thought I had done a darn good job selling that night until years later, when I buried the wife. The husband told me the only reason I had made the sale was because I was such a good sport about the wine. People love to laugh, even when it is during making advanced arrangements for their deaths. Laughter is like cream in coffee- it floats to the top.

Sometimes, customers cause me to laugh. One night, I had an appointment in Cape Coral. As I drove up to their home in an exclusive neighborhood in my 1969 Barracuda with no a/c, I saw in their driveway two matching Cadillacs. One car sported the husband's name on the tags; the other, the wife's. I said to myself, "Lee, you don't belong here." But I bit my tongue and knocked on the door, anyway.

"Darling! Welcome!" Mrs. Brown threw her arms around me. She and her husband welcomed me like an old, lost friend. It was my first big sale, and I gave her a textbook sales pitch. I offered them ground burial or the more expensive crypt internment. They chose the crypt internment and didn't blink an eye when they paid cash for the rather large transaction.

"Now, do that again, darling."

"Do what?" I asked mystified.

"Why your closing sales pitch, of course. I'm going to real estate school and I like your closing. Do it again."

I stifled my laughter, took a deep breath, and like an obedient child, did it again. Mrs. Brown got her real estate license and the last I heard was quite successful. I wonder if she's still using my closing.

After about a year of sales, I was made sales manager. I had a motley crew, some I had hired; some I had inherited. I hired an old, retired Navy buddy who had a bizarre sense of humor. One day, I received a call that everyone was laughing when they came from the Mausoleum chapel. I went to see what could be so funny in a cemetery. There was my Navy buddy holding a big sign that read, "Last Crypt, Buy Today."

Putting on a poker face, I sternly reprimanded him reminding him we were not a used car lot. But I was dying of laughter, inside. He could tell by my eyes I thought it was funny, but for the sake of propriety, he put the sign away and things returned to "normal" if there is such a thing in a cemetery.

Another one of my salesmen who actually turned out to be my best producer, took me on a sales call with him so I could rate his job performance. He knocked on the door and took off his shoes. I thought to myself, "Is this guy nuts?" Before I could say anything, the door opened and my salesman explained to the hostess that back in Alabama where he came from, it was customary to remove one's shoes before entering a home so as not to track in dirt.

My shoeless cemetery plot salesman introduced me as a trainee and I sat on the couch to observe. Actually, I was too shocked to do anything else! After he made his presentation , they said they wanted to think about it.

"What did I do wrong, M'am?" He accentuated his Southern drawl. "If I go back without a sale my boss will think I don't know how to sell. I know good people like you will be able to help me." He smiled broadly and really laid on the Southern charm.

The couple reviewed his sales pitch with him, much like parents helping a child with his homework. They talked themselves right into buying two spaces from him. The last I heard of him, he had his own cemetery in Pensacola. A man can dig his way up to the top, even in the cemetery business!

After a few years of doing very well in sales, I was promoted to General Manager and then to Vice-President of the corporation. The sales manager I hired was so afraid of the cemetery, he wouldn't go there after dark. It might seem like he was in the wrong business, but I had a "feeling" about him when I hired him. He was an insurance man in Ohio and got tired of the ice and the snow. He packed his golf clubs and came to Florida. He told his wife and kids he would send for them when he got a job. I liked his commitment and hired him. He was with me for eight years and was a story by himself. I've devoted a whole section under "Employees" to my "spooked" sales manager for the reader's pleasure.

A few situations arose that I want to refer to as "The Traveling Deceased." In 1989, a fellow came to see me at the cemetery, and said that he wanted to bury his father-in-law. We went into my office to make burial arrangements.

"Where did your father-in-law die?"

"In Alabama."

"Where is the body?"

"In the back of my pick-up truck."

I will remember forever my shock when Mr. William Brinks told me how he traveled from Alabama (his home) to Southwest Florida with Joseph P. Walters in the bed of his truck. I made a few phone calls and found out he did everything legally, so we made the burial in our Veterans Garden. I mean, after all, he was stiff enough to salute!

Sixteen years after the burial, the deceased's daughter, Cindy came in to see me about applying for her father's military medals. She didn't remember me, and was surprised I remembered her. But how can you forget a family whose father was brought in for burial in the back of a pick-up truck? We had a few laughs. The more years that pass, the funnier it gets.

A few years later, a lady walked in the front door and said she wanted to make arrangements to bury her husband.

"Where can we pick up the body?" I asked.

"In the front seat of my car. We were traveling to our winter home in Fort Myers and he died on the way. Around Sarasota, I think. Since we were coming to Fort Myers, anyway, I just thought I'd bring him the rest of the way."

There's another one along for the ride. I wonder if dead people are good company? They can't argue with you while you're driving, and they never interrupt your train of thought. And they certainly aren't backseat drivers. Maybe, these people aren't as crazy as they seem.

In this introduction, I've provided the candy coating to the funny side of death. Now get ready to die from laughing. Well, not really, I wouldn't want to have to bury the reader, too!

THE SINGLE LIFE

DRIVING THINGS HOME

When I had the cemetery in Lehigh Acres, and was single and just starting out in the business, I couldn't afford a car AND a hearse, so I used a hearse for my transportation. I was working even when I was playing. When I was out for a night on the town, invariably, I would get beeped to pick up a body (make a removal) or have to go see a family for pre-arrangements, etc. I always had on my suit or sports coat so as to be well prepared.

A lot of people kidded me about not relaxing, but I was always afraid to let my hair down. I could just see someone saying, "That joker, HE'S going to be burying my loved one?" So I always had my work face on, even when I was playing. A few times, I was asked by friends to park the hearse down the street and not in front of their houses.

The hearse came in handy one time when I was having lunch at the Nineteenth Hole next to the golf course. A golfer was clutching his chest, so I ran down to help.

"I think he's having a heart attack." His friend said. "Should I call an ambulance?" This was before the days of cell phones.

"No, it would take too long to walk up and make the call. And then you'd have to wait for the ambulance to get here. I'll just take him. I'm parked close by." His friend helped me get the golfer to the hearse.

3

"I'm going to the hospital in a hearse?" the golfer asked incredulously. "Now I know I'm going to die."

"You're not going to die. It's the fastest way there." I ran a few red lights and made a few sharp turns, but I got him there in time and he lived. I guess my motto during this period of my life was, "Have hearse, will travel."

BUY NOW, PAY LATER

I opened one of the first, if not the very first, Shopping Center Casket Stores. In the mid 80's, I rented a storefront in Homosassa Springs, Florida, and started selling Pre-Need Services, caskets, monuments, etc. It was received pretty well by the general population, except the local funeral directors didn't like the competition and thought I was breaking the law. The business I felt sorry for was the Arthur Murray dance studio next door. The old folks going in for dancing lessons didn't like seeing caskets at night when they went in for their sessions. So, I tinted my windows, and they were happy with me.

The one I didn't make happy was the restaurant owner at the end of the mall. He came to my door, flung it open, and spewed his venom. "Mr. Downs, it is obscene showing this stuff in public and you should be closed down!" He stormed.

"Don't you have the Italian Restaurant?" I asked politely.

"Yes, I have a RESPECTABLE business."

"You should be put out of business for competing with Italian mammas that make much better food than you ever will. Besides, I hate restaurant Italian food."

He threw up his hands, mumbled something in Italian and marched out. Needless to say, I never heard any more from him. The casket store idea caught on, and many stores have opened up across the country.

THE DEAD END CEMETERY

When I had my cemetery in Homosassa, Florida, it was located at the end of a street. The only way to make a U-turn was in the circle of the cemetery entrance which contained a pond flanked by benches and flags. People were always flying down the road and coming to a screeching halt when they realized it wasn't a THRU road. Some even skidded up to the pond. One motorcyclist even ended up in the pond.

That was the straw that broke the camel's back. I went to the county commissioners to get a sign placed. They put up a sign that read DEAD END. Of course, I started getting a lot of comments and jokes about the Dead End cemetery. After I lobbied the commissioners again, they replaced the Dead End sign with one that read NO THRU WAY, and they had a few good chuckles at my expense.

LET YOUR LIGHT SHINE SO I KNOW YOU'RE REAL

When I was single, I lived in the cemetery in my travel trailer. There were a number of occasions for a laugh about me living in the dead part of town. Some people actually thought I lived among the dead, and wasn't real, myself. People that lived in Immokalee, which is the next city over from my cemetery, would stop by the cemetery in the evening on the way home from shopping in Fort Myers.

One night, I noticed people by a grave on their knees and not knowing whether they were visiting a loved one or whether they were vandals, I decided to check it out. It was pitch dark when I walked up behind them.

"Can I help you?" My voice broke the silence of the night.

"Ahhhhhh!" The woman in the party on her knees screamed and fell forward on the grave.

"It's O.K.!" I said hurriedly. "I'm Lee Downs, the owner of the cemetery." The woman regained her composure with the help of her teen-age children who were too scared to say anything.

"Don't be sneaking up behind people in the dark, Mr. Downs." The woman scolded. "You nearly gave me a heart attack."

"Yes, M'am." I smiled sheepishly. So from that day forward, I decided to alert people that I was coming with a flashlight. I only have to be yelled at once before I learn. Ask my wife.

MY FAMILY

Thе Romance of the Grave

Funeral homes can be wildly romantic and intimate places. In the chapel of my funeral home, we had a beautiful stained glass window. Everybody in town would ride by and comment on it. It was truly striking. Over a period of time, I married three couples under that stained glass window. In fact, my wife, Fran and I were also married under that stained glass window by a very good friend of mine and his wife took the video. Other good friends, John Jones and his wife, stood up for us. We got married on my wife's birthday, December 11th. I guess there will always be a soft spot in our hearts for this chapel of romance in our funeral home in Lehigh Acres.

We told our friends to keep our marriage a secret until we announced it at our annual Christmas party in two weeks. Our annual Christmas party was an event that all my friends looked forward to. I would have it at the Matador Room in Lehigh Acres. We had steak, shrimp and all the works. Both of my buddies were well known in the community and among the golfers, so I was sure everyone would find out. We wore our rings and didn't try to hide them. But to my surprise, the day of the Christmas Party no one knew or had found out. Our announcement was a little Christmas present to all of our friends!

Some of my funeral directors would refer business to my cemetery, and then say, "Can I get a better steak, now?" Well, the day we announced our wedding, everybody got a better steak!

☊✟☊

When I got into the funeral business, I began thinking about what were the final wishes and desires of my own loved ones. One night over a family supper, I asked my mother, "Mom, what kind of funeral arrangements do you want?"

"Oh, I don't know. Cremate me." She was feeding her favorite dachshund, Snoopy, bits of choice roast beef under the table. He licked her hand in appreciation and whined for more.

"But if I die before Snoopy, I want you to put him to sleep and cremate him with me." She petted his head, and scratched him behind the ear.

"Mom, I'll be glad to honor your wishes," I said seriously. "But if Snoopy dies first, should I put you to sleep and cremate you with him?"

"Oh Lee!" She reprimanded as the rest of the family at the table burst out laughing. She never asked me about that again.

Since that evening, mom has reconsidered. Now I am to cremate her and put her in four urns for each child to sprinkle when they travel. My mom is a world traveler. She even took a cruise when she got out of the hospital this year. My sister went with her and attended to her like a nurse. There was no way my mom was going to miss the boat!

Mom has always one-upped me when she travels. She went to Spain before I had a chance to get there, courtesy of the

U.S. Navy. And she's been lots of places that I haven't been yet, including Russia and Jerusalem. Well, even after she passes, she'll still be one-upping me travelling everywhere the four winds can carry her. And I'm sure she'll tell me all about it in the afterlife, as she's petting her pet dog, Snoopy!

THE SHINING

When I had my cemetery in Homosassa, Florida, my son was maintenance manager. He had a son that was about nine years old. We called him " Little Lee" because his mother had named him, "Ian," and I didn't much care to say "Ian." It always reminded me of sissy English actors.

Well, Little Lee would walk the cemetery. If he saw visitors, he would approach them and say, "This is my grandfather's cemetery, and if you want to know anything I can help you." Because he was a little boy who seemed to appear out of nowhere, the startled visitors weren't sure if he wasn't one of the residents of the cemetery. But after they got over their initial fright, Little Lee was very helpful in directing them where they wanted to go. We called him our unofficial tour guide.

MY SON, TERRY ~ A CHIP OFF THE OLD CASKET

TERRY AND THE GOLD BALL

Before I sold my cemetery in Homosassa, a man came in to make prearrangements. We drew up a standard package and then he said, "One more thing- I have a 14 ounce gold ball behind my glass eye. I want it removed and returned to my wife before I'm cremated."

I thought he was pulling my leg, and then I looked at him closely, and noticed he did have a glass eye.

"Wouldn't a bank or a safe deposit box be a safer place for that?" I asked.

"How much safer can I get than behind my eye? Even if somebody did find out about it, they'd have to pop my eyeball out to get it. And believe me, ain't nobody going to do that while I'm alive!"

So, I swallowed my laughter and wrote in arrangements to have the gold ball removed at his death. Well, as it goes I sold the cemetery and my son, Terry stayed on to run the cemetery for the new owners. A few months later, I was at my funeral home in Lehigh Acres (about 200 miles South), when my son called all excited.

"Dad, this guy died and he has a gold ball behind his eye, and the family wants me to remove it!"

"Yea, I forgot to tell you about that. Just pop out the eye, and clean the ball. Then give it to his wife."

"That's gross. I'm not going to do that."

"You have to, son. It's part of the job." I explained. Terry hung up grumbling. He went and had a few beers and called me back.

"Dad, you come up and do it. You're use to stuff like this."

" I can't Terry. It's too far, and I have responsibilities here. Just do it."

He was still grumbling when he hung up. After a few more beers and some time later, my son called me again.

"Dad, I asked the funeral director to do it."

"Did he?"

"No, he said it wasn't his case and he wasn't doing it. Then he laughed and said, 'Didn't your Daddy tell you there would be days like this?'"

Terry called one last time. "I did it! It was ugly and covered with green slime, but I reached in there and got that sucker. I cleaned it up and gave it to the wife. But I'm telling you, Dad. I'm never doing anything like that again!"

Yes, he will. You do what you have to in life. And this was probably the biggest lesson Terry learned.

TERRY AND "BABY"

Adjacent to my cemetery in Homosassa, I owned a pet cemetery. People get so emotionally attached to their animals, pet internment can be a big business.

One day, an older Spinster school teacher came into my office to talk to me about her dog.

"Oh, Mr. Downs," she cried. "My dog, 'Baby' is in intensive care. I just spent $26,000 dollars on him and he's not going to live."

"I'm so sorry, Miss Oliver." I comforted. But what I really was thinking was, " $26,000 dollars! That's enough to put my kid through college!" She was really committed to bringing up Baby!" When I had recovered from the shock of her spending that much on a dog, she hit me with more.

"I'm here to make arrangements for his funeral. Baby weighs 150 pounds.

I involuntarily made a low, soft whistle. "Miss Oliver, you will need a full size casket and four pet spaces for a dog that size."

"No problem. Baby's family." And with that she pulled out her checkbook and wrote a check for the full amount.

A few days later, Baby died. The animal hospital had sent Baby home to die. Baby died in the middle of the kitchen floor. I sent my son, Terry, to pick him up. After Terry got there, he called.

"Dad, do you know how big this dog is?"

"Yea, but I wasn't thinking dead weight. I'll send a couple of guys to help you."

Terry hung up, but I heard what happened later. The help arrived, but Miss Oliver insisted on staying in the kitchen while they picked the dog up.

"O.K., Fred, I've got the rear. You get the head, and John, you grab the middle." Terry directed.

"Don't hurt my Baby!" Miss Oliver lamented.

"M'am, there ain't no way we can hurt this dog." Terry said while heaving his guts out. The men lifted their parts. Terry backed into a kitchen island and dropped the rear. It landed on the floor with a resounding thud.

"You dropped my Baby!" Miss Oliver cried.

"I'm sorry, M'am. It will be O.K. He won't bruise." Terry apologized. Miss Oliver ran from the room in distress. The boys took this opportunity to finish putting the dog in the body bag, and with much trouble, carried the dog out to the truck. Terry went back in, and soothed Miss Oliver's feathers.

"I'm going to have a full funeral for Baby. Only the best for my Baby." Miss Oliver declared.

"That's really great, M'am." Terry cajoled.

"See you at the funeral!"

"Err.... Yea, see you at the funeral."

This goes to show, pets can be as dear as children to some people. Everyone needs someone in his or her life. Even if that "someone" has four feet and a shaggy tail!

ARMY UNIFORMS AREN'T THE ONLY THINGS THAT ARE GREEN

A few months after we had buried this gentleman, his family came in and requested that we disinter him and dress him in his Army uniform. We tried to discourage the disturbing of the dead, and told them the vault would have to be replaced. The cost of the vault and our services, along with the cemetery charges would be expensive. They didn't care. Dad had been in the Army for thirty years and should have his uniform on.

My son, Terry, had never done a disinterment before and was apprehensive. He really is a babe in the woods, sometimes. We cracked the bottom of the Vault.

"Dad!" Terry yelled. "There's fluid running out on my tennis shoes! And don't you smell the odor?"

"Son, that's normal." I could see Terry was as green as the Army uniform we brought to put on the deceased.

"Here, take a break. Have a cigar." I offered.

"Dad, you know I don't smoke." He said as he lit the end. He puffed on it pretty strongly, and soon the only thing we could smell was the cigar odor. The deceased, being an Army sergeant, would have said, "Smoke 'em while you got 'em, boys." We removed the sergeant's suit and put his uniform on. We made a Polaroid of him for his family, and they were very happy, feeling Dad was truly at rest, now. And Terry's color returned to normal, after only a few hours!

flat chance

Sometimes, I had to send my staff to another state to pick up a body for burial in Homosassa. Once, I sent my son, Terry, my seven year-old grandson, Billy and an employee named Fred to disinter a vault in Georgia and bring the body back. Here's the story as my son tells it:

We left Homosassa early Thursday in a 1959 Chevy flatbed with a hoist on the back that surely wasn't designed for a truck that small. In fact, I think the hoist weighed as much as the truck. We had an unlimited expense account- as much as a platinum Texaco card could hold. That card got abused. Thanks Dad, for the card.

I drove, Billy sat in the middle and Fred rode shot gun. Now nothing rattled Fred. He was a man in his 50's with a gray beard who smoked a pipe. We had eight flat tires before we reached North Georgia.

Each time we had one, the conversation went like this:

"Damn it, Fred." I complained. "We've got another flat tire."

"Yep." Fred took a nice long draw on his pipe. "Think we better pull over." We would change the tire and then look for a service station to get the flat fixed. Fred just kept puffing on his pipe and listened to country music on the radio. As far as he was concerned, it was like we were out for a Sunday drive in the country.

We finally reached North Georgia. Finding the cemetery and the burial site was the easiest part of the trip. Digging a vault and casket out of Georgia red clay is an experience everyone should try at least once. The suction from the moist clay and the weight of the vault only caused the front of the truck to rise in the air and the vault to stay firmly implanted. Fred and I talked about it, and being the industrious Florida boys that we were, we found some stones and old wood to support the back of the truck and finally got the vault loose. All the while, Fred just kept sucking on that pipe, not saying much about anything.

The trip back was really fun. We left Georgia late Saturday night. That platinum Texaco card would not get us a room at the Comfort Inn, so we stopped at a roadside rest stop. Now, three people cannot sleep in the front of a '59 Chevy truck, so I elected to sleep on the hood of the truck. About 3 a.m., I was awakened by a rather severe thunderstorm, and spent the rest of the night squeezed into the driver's side, until they woke up.

Almost home, we got our ninth, maybe tenth flat tire. We pulled into the ever present Texaco station in a neighborhood of color in the middle of the night. I bet we were the only white people they had ever seen with a vault with a dead person in it, a six year old platinum Texaco card and a flat tire. The locals refused to get near the dead body on the truck, but they gave us full use of the shop to fix the truck, and in the end, they didn't even charge us anything. They were just glad to see our taillights leaving their town!

When we got back to work, Dad asked Fred how it went. Fred took a long draw on his pipe and said, "It was just an average trip, Lee. Nothing special."

FLIP ME OVER WHEN I'M DONE ON THIS SIDE

We couldn't cremate anyone until we had the proper clearance from the medical examiner and we had to wait 48 hours. This one week-end, (it was a long holiday week-end), everyone was anxious to go home, including my son, Terry, who was the crematory operator at the time. After checking the proper paperwork, Terry turned on the crematory for Mr. Williams. He then came up to my office to tell me he was on his last job.

I was on the phone with Mrs. Williams.

"Mr. Downs, we've changed our mind about the cremation. We want to have a viewing and a funeral."

"No problem, Mrs. Williams. We haven't done anything, yet." Terry began to motion wildly that we had. I hung up with Mrs. Williams and Terry and I raced down to the crematory. Terry got there first, and stopped the machine. I checked out Mr. Williams. He was a little warm, but no damage was done. We stored Mr. Williams, and left for our well-deserved holiday week-end.

THE TWO PIERRES

I have run into some strange situations in my career, but none were stranger than the case of the Two Pierres. The widow of the first Pierre was motivated by love of love. The widow of the second Pierre was motivated by love of money. It is my hope that both widows and both Pierres provide some comic relief.

The FIRST PIERRE

"Is this Mr. Downs?"

"Speaking."

"Don't think I'm crazy but I was told to call you by the Fort Myers Funeral Home."

I waited because any conversation that starts out with 'Don't think I'm crazy' usually gives me ample reason to think just that. This was no exception.

"My husband is in a casket stored at the funeral home. I go to see him on a regular basis, and have for four years, now."

"O.K., lady, you've had your fun." I sighed. "But I am much too busy for jokes."

"No, Mr. Downs, I'm serious." The woman's voice took on a pleading quality. "You've got to help me."

I made an appointment with Mrs. Roman for the following day, and wondered what kind of a woman kept her husband "stored" at a funeral home. I found out later it was the kind of woman who was crazy in love. Love can make us do all sorts of wild, insane things. And Mrs. Roman was no exception.

"You say you 'visit' your husband at the funeral home." I started. "What do they do? Raise the lid whenever you want to take a peak?"

"No, I purchased a glass top sealed casket. I go to see him at least once a month, and I'm paying the funeral home rent." She explained.

"Oh." I said letting this information sink in, and trying to maintain an attitude that this was perfectly normal. "Well, it sounds like you got a nice set-up there. What do you need from me?" I asked sincerely.

"I want to buy a crypt so I can bury him, yet still be able to see him."

This was a bit unusual but I sold her a crypt and agreed not to seal it so we could slide the casket out and view Pierre. I charged her $100 dollars every time she came out to see him. She spent better than $100,000 dollars for the whole project back in the "70's.

One day she came to view Pierre, and I escorted her to the crypt and pulled him out for her.

"Oh, he hasn't changed a bit since last week!" She exclaimed.

"Yes, m'am," I said wondering how she expected a dead man to change.

"See that mole above his lip?" She pointed.

"Yes, ma'm."

"It changes size every time I come to see him." She explained. "That's why I was so surprised it hadn't changed... wait a minute. I think it's a little bigger this week. Yes, yes it is."

After a goodly amount of time had passed, I found out that she was remarried and that her husband was in the construction business. I spoke to her next time she came in.

"Why don't you get your new husband to build a room on the side of the house for Pierre?" I asked. "It would save you a lot of money."

"Oh Lee," she whispered. "My new husband doesn't know I do this. In fact, no one in the family knows I do this."

All this secrecy made it sound like she was having an affair with a dead guy. I guess, in a way, she was having an affair with a dead guy.

"When I die, I want no ceremony, no service, nothing. Just put me next to Pierre. I'll even pre-pay."

And she did. This was all such a secret from her husband and family, she wouldn't even allow me to put the nameplate on the crypt until after she died.

When she died, we did what is called a "direct burial." She was put into a cardboard casket and put in the crypt with Pierre. Her new husband was upset, but the course of true love takes many odd twists and turns in life-- and in death!

THE SECOND PIERRE

Mr. Rivera was stored in the cooler at my funeral home in Lehigh Acres for eleven years. Mrs. Rivera did not want him buried. She had some kind of a lawsuit with the city of Fort Myers over the cause of his death. He was embalmed and placed in a special casket that could be opened for viewings and further examinations. Examiners would come in accompanied by Mrs. Rivera.

"O.K., boys. Get your piece of skin or pound of flesh." Mrs. Rivera said breezily. She patted the dead man's arm. "Pierre, darling- you're going to make me a millionaire." She smiled.

This was a regular event for the first couple of years. Then everyone seemed to forget about poor Pierre while his wife fought with the lawyers. In the eleventh year, Mrs. Rivera was fighting with an executive of the insurance company. He looked at the death certificate and asked where Pierre was buried. She said, "He's not. He's in the cooler at Anderson Funeral Home."

The next day I got a call from the St. Petersburg Times.

"Mr. Downs, is it true you have a body stored in your cooler for eleven years?"

"Well, yes."

"Why?"

"The body was involved in a lawsuit."

"But did you need to keep the body for eleven years?"

"It was the wish of the wife."

Now that the press was involved, I called my partner, Ron Anderson.

"Ron, Mr. Rivera's story has leaked out. The press wants to know why we've had Pierre on ice so long."

"Because he would smell terribly if we didn't have him on ice."

"Don't be funny, Ron. You're going to have to deal with the news people because this is your case."

"But it's your funeral home. You handle it."

"Gee thanks, Ron."

The next morning, I had newspaper reporters, CBS News, and local T.V. people all waiting at my office door.

"Mr. Downs, tell us about Pierre."

"Why have you had him eleven years?"

"What do you plan to do with the body?"

"Can we see Pierre?"

And this was all before I could get my office door open. Pierre had become a celebrity overnight.

"Can we get in the cooler to see Pierre?"

"No, I can't allow that." I tried to field their questions.

"Can we at least take pictures of you in front of the cooler and pictures of the funeral home?"

"Yes, I suppose that would be O.K." I posed for them in front of all the prime locations, and being a little vain, turned so they would get my best side. I wanted my wife and mother to be proud.

Looking into the case, after the reporters left for the day, I found that Mrs. Rivera owed $100,000 dollars in back charges. I called her about it.

"I know I owe it, Lee. But the insurance company has never paid me, so I can't afford to pay it."

"But surely you don't need the body anymore. I mean, they must have gotten all the samples they need."

"Yes, that's true. But I can't afford to bury Pierre, either."

"If I forgive all the charges, can I bury him?"

"Honey, if you forgive all the charges, Pierre's all yours!"

So, I made arrangements with a friend of mine at the Florida National Cemetery in Bushnell to bury him. My friend thought I was nuts but agreed to set it up. My wife and I took Pierre to the cemetery in the hearse and we were followed by 60 Minutes cameras. I guess we were quite a circus with the hearse in the lead and all the news people following us. But at last, Pierre finally got to rest in peace.

The really funny side to this was my son, Terry, was in a bar in Fort Pierce, Florida, and was looking at the news on T.V. when the 60 Minutes story came on.

"Hey, your old man is in the funeral business, isn't he?" Terry's friend asked as he raised his beer.

"Yea, in fact, dad's got a body stored like that."

"No kidding? Is that common?"

"Nothing is common for my father."

"The newscaster just said 'Lehigh Acres.'" Terry's friend said. At that moment they showed me getting out of the hearse.

"That IS my father." Terry gulped.

I know Terry wonders why I can't hold a normal job like other fathers- a mailman, police officer, or store clerk. But life is always exciting for him, even when he's out of town!

THE CLERGY

FATHER LIMA

Father Lima O'Roarke was a very, strict, Irish-Catholic priest. Whatever he said had to be heeded. It was his way or no way. For instance, when I called him to do a service on Saturday, we would have to do the mass at 10 a.m. We had to get to the cemetery and back by 11 a.m., in time for his wine and cigar time. I would say, "But the family wants it at eleven." He would reply, "I only do it at ten, boy."

It took me a while to get on his good side. He always insisted on standing in the covey of the chapel because it had a big cross there. But it had no light there.

"Father, there is a light and a podium in the front of the chapel. Why don't you use that?"

"I only stand by the cross, boy."

I made him real happy one day. My chapel at the cemetery was an open air, outdoor chapel. I had the electrician hook up a light above the cross. Father Lima came in and noticed the light right away.

"Lee, you Southern Baptist Catholic! Have one of my cigars!" He offered. It was nasty, but we were friends from that day on.

In one of our wine and cigar chats, I found out how he got his first name.

"How did a good Irish boy like you get a name like 'Lima?'" I asked him one day.

"Me mother was in love with St. Rose of Lima. So much so, that she vowed her next child would be named after the saint. Her next child was a boy..... me. Now, you can imagine the stir it would have created to have an altar boy named, 'Rose', so she decided to name me 'Lima.' And confidentially, I am damn glad, boy."

Father Lima caused quite a stir one day. I always met funerals from different funeral homes at the main gate and escorted them to the gravesite. After the funeral director and I would get the casket on the lowering device, I would escort the family and the clergy to the gravesite. On the way to the site, I would explain to the clergy which was the head of the grave.

One of my gardens, the Garden of Prophecy had Surinam Cherry hedges. One day we had a gravesite next to a hedge and I warned Father Lima not to go to the head of the grave but to stand by the casket because he might fall into the grave.

"I always go to the head of the casket, boy." He said indignantly. I listened and watched.

Our brother, Joe, will rise again on the last day." Father preached. He took a step backwards and fell into the grave. Everyone wanted to laugh, but if you knew Father Lima, you knew you had better not laugh. Now, it was no easy task getting Father Lima out of that grave. We had to move the casket and the lowering device, pull Father Lima out, and set everything back like it was.

Father Lima brushed himself off, and looked like a bull cooling down after a rodeo ride. He looked at the small congregation that were eating their giggles. "And that's exactly how Joe will be risen on the last day!" He finished his service and left.

After he left, the funeral director and I who had maintained our composure beautifully through all this, lost it, as did many of the family members, and belly laughs could be heard coming from the gravesite. I am sure Joe would have approved, although Father Lima would not have.

Another day, we were scheduled to have a Catholic funeral. My assistant was a devout Catholic and knew the family. He warned me to have smelling salts available. Little did we know that the whole front row of the assembly of family and friends were professional wailers.

All through the service, they kept standing and moaning, "Ahh, Mamma don't go! Don't go! We need you! Don't go!" Father Lima snapped his fingers, leaned over and whispered, "That's enough of that crap!" They knew he meant business, so they sat down and Father Lima finished his service. If it were up to the professional wailers, it would have been hours before the woman was in the ground. Whether you liked Father Lima or hated Father Lima, he was always himself, pasturing his flock in this life and moving his sheep into the next.

FATHER GUN

Father Gun was a real pistol. He was a funny, half-blind priest with an eye for the ladies, although he said he just appreciated looking at God's creations.

Father Gun loved a good joke. When he came to the funeral home for an evening wake service, he came to the office. At first, he would be all business and get the family information. Then, his sense of humor would come out and he'd start telling jokes or made me tell him new ones I've heard. We would laugh like hyenas until time for the service. Then, he would put on his poker face and go out and console the family.

After the service, he would turn his collar around or remove it, and climb into his convertible.

"Good night, Lee."

"Where are you headed, Father?"

"The beach."

"Again? Father, I know you're watching the girls on the boardwalk."

"Man does not live by bread alone, my son. Besides, I pray at the beach."

"Pray for a woman, I bet."

"Only the Lord knows what I pray for." Father Gun raised an eyebrow.

Father Gun was a very popular clergy because of his sense of humor. He always got the job done, but had a few good laughs along the way.

WhEN ThE SAINTS COME MARChING IN

My son, Terry worked for me at my cemetery in Homosassa, Florida. He was in charge of the crematory, and had to make the removal of dead bodies. Well, back then, we only had beepers. This was in the days well before cell phones. For those that don't remember those times, a beeper was a device you wore on your belt. It made an obnoxiously loud "Beep! Beep!" followed by an obnoxiously loud message.

One Sunday morning, I was in church. The preacher was giving his sermon.

"On the last day, the Lord will pick our bodies up from the grave and raise them to heaven." The preacher said with passion.

At that moment, my beeper went off, followed by my son saying, "I'm going to Homosassa to pick up a body. Will get back to you, Later."

Everything got real quiet in the church, and I wondered if some people didn't think it was the Lord talking. Embarrassed,

I smiled and went outside to answer him, leaving the preacher to top that in his sermon.

NERVOUS NELLIE

We allowed churches that were just starting out or had a small congregation to meet in our chapel at the funeral home. The only thing I required was that they would clean and vacuum for me. One church was a small Black Baptist group. The minister said he would like to use my chapel because they couldn't afford to pay rent at the senior center. I agreed to let them meet in the chapel.

However, he had one member of his congregation, an elderly woman, who was dead set against meeting in a funeral home. He brought Nellie over to see the place and to talk to me.

"Now, Nellie, as you can see, my chapel has a big, stained glass window in front and pews. It looks like a real church."

"What about all the dead bodies?"

"When you come to church on Sunday, you come here to the chapel. You don't have to go anywhere else in the funeral home."

"What about ghosts?"

"There are no ghosts that are going to hurt you. Besides, if you believe in Our Lord, you know you're protected whether you're home in your living room or whether you're here."

She finally agreed, and they started having services in our chapel. Up to the day we sold the funeral home, they were still there. Nellie never did trust completely, though. Sometimes, I would go in on Sunday to check on something in the office, and every time I peeked into the chapel, I would see her in the back pews, always looking over her shoulder.

FAMOUS PEOPLE

When I travel, one of my hobbies is to visit cemeteries and locate famous graves. I keep a book with locations of the graves and pictures of each. I'll never forget the first time I took my new wife, Fran, to a famous person's grave. It was the grave of Hank Williams in Montgomery, Alabama.

After climbing into the car I said, "Got everything for the trip, honey?"

" I'm not sure, Lee," fretted Fran. "What do you take on a trip to a dead country western superstar's grave?"

"Oh, just yourself and your camera." I consoled.

"You know, people don't believe that I dated and married someone that drives a hearse and takes me to cemeteries."

"You make me sound like Herman Munster."

"Well?" Fran laughed.

We liked to travel in our motor home to visit our children who are scattered across the nation. Once, I combined my hobby with visiting my wife's daughter, Cindy, in Atlanta, Georgia. Cindy had just had a new baby, her first child. She was all full of life and new motherhood. Cindy was thinking about cute baby clothes and non-lactose baby formulas when I loaded her and Fran into the car to go for a ride outside of Atlanta to Carrolton to see Susan Haywards' grave.

"What the hell am I doing looking at dead people with a new baby?" Cindy exclaimed.

"You're not going to see just any dead person. " I calmed her down. "You're going to see Susan Haywards."

"So?"

"You're too young to know who Susan was, but I always had a crush on her. " I sighed.

"I never knew you had a thing for Susan Haywards." Fran pondered.

"I'll tell you a little secret, Fran. Susan never knew it, either."

When Elvis Aaron Presley died, I accidentally became a bit of a celebrity, myself. Elvis may have left the building, but I didn't. When Graceland opened for fans to view the King's body, in August, 1977, guess who was the first one at the entrance waiting to get in?

I stood at the gate for eight hours holding my wife's and mother's hands. I made the front page of T.V. Guide, Rolling Stone Magazine, and we were in the last three of his biographical movies. We also had the same picture in a number of books about Elvis. I may have been the first of the public to see the body, but I was not "lonesome tonight" because the crowd was unbelievable.

Another famous person I came into contact with was Jackie Gleason's third wife, Marilyn. I got the contract to sell the marble for Jackie Gleason's crypt in Miami. I was the Georgia Marble representative for Florida, and when his wife came in to build his crypt, we got to sell the marble. He had $150,000 dollars in his will for the building. The crypt has three stairs up to the sarcophagus of Jackie, and they say, "And away we go." I often wondered how many pall bearers it took to get Jackie up those three stairs. He was no light weight.

Coincidently, my step-father is buried in the same cemetery across the pond from Jackie. Of course, his grave has nowhere near the splendor of Jackie's but he does have one thing in common with Jackie. They're both dead. Death comes to the rich and the poor alike and everyone in between. So you might as well roll with the punches and laugh while you can.

My hobby has led me all over the country. I've got pictures of Marilyn Monroe's crypt, Alan Ladd, Walt Disney, Dorothy Stratton, Natalie Wood, and others. Some graves are simple. Errol Flynn just has a simple government bronze marker. Some, like Jackie's are really elaborate. People's choices for their final resting place have given me quite a collection of pictures.

I've buried a few famous people in my time. I was in my office at the cemetery one day when this gentleman came in to purchase burial spaces for his wife. He seemed like he wanted to talk a bit more than just the usual information for burial, so I sat down with him and chatted.

"Can I smoke?" He asked shyly.

"Of course, I'll join you." At that time, I used to smoke Muriel Coronella cigars. I pulled a cigar out of my desk.

"That's my wife!" He exclaimed looking at the box.

"Your wife?" I questioned.

"Yes, when she was younger she made a portfolio of her pictures to try and get work as a model. One of the pictures was her with a veil on her face. She gave her pictures to the wrong guy." He sighed. "An unscrupulous photographer who ended up selling them and she never got a dime." He shook his head.

"I'm sorry." I offered.

"Not that it matters now. Money won't do her any good now. So enjoy it while you got it."

The man made sense.

Another famous person I buried was Cora Fiedler from the Arthur Fiedler family. Rich people bury just like regular folks only they have a few more bells and whistles.

I HAD TO SHOW THE GREEN AT GREEN AND WEST'S CONCERT

One year, at the National Cemetery Convention, I had a front row table at the final night banquet. It was a dinner and a show. At my table was Dianne, a well known supplier of cemetery bronze markers. Suppliers customarily wined and dined us buyers. We thought Dianne was no exception.

"Waitress!" Dianne called in a typical New York accent. "Bring a bottle of your most expensive red wine for this table. Break out the good stuff!" I was impressed.

"So, Lee, Ya goin' to see that country music singer- What's his name, Elvis? In Memphis?" Dianne wasn't much on music but she did know her bronze and cemetery markers.

"Yes, Dianne, I'm going to see him. He's a great singer."

Dianne's date was sitting directly across from her, and I think they were playing footies. Dianne had her shoe off, and having had a little too much to drink, mistakenly touched my ankle instead of his.

Dottie West and Jack Green, famous country-western music stars took the stage, and the show was starting. Dianne stood up and said to her date, "Come on, Ron. Let's blow this joint. I hate country-western." They strode off with arms entwined around each other.

It was a good show. Then the waitress brought the bill. I got stuck paying for that expensive bottle of wine all because of Dianne's taste in music- and in men!

MY PHOTO ALBUM

We were married in the chapel in our funeral home on my wife's birthday, Dec. 11, 1990.

Charlie Matheny married us and his wife Willie took pictures.

Bob and Marylou Craven stood up for us.

*I was the first one in the house to see the
body of Elvis, August 17, 1977.*

Marilyn, Jackie Gleason's 3rd wife and Joe Robbie.

Scale model of Jackie Gleason's mausoleum.

Elvis Aaron Presley, January 8, 1935 - August 16, 1977, Graceand, Memphis, TN.

Susan Hayward, June 30, 1917 - March 14, 1975.

Hank Snow, May 9, 1914 - December 20, 1999, Nashville, TN.

Rex Allen Museum, Wilcox, Arizona.

Floyd Cramer, October 27, 1933 -
December 31, 1997, Nashville, TN.

Stan Laurel, June 16, 1890 - February 23, 1965.

Grace Allen Burns, July 26, 1895 - August 27, 1964.

Alan Ladd, 1913 - 1964.

Ernest Taylor Pyle, August 3, 1900 - April 18, 1945.

Merle Kilgore - Hendersonville, TN. Grave Next to Johnny Cash. August 9, 1934 - February 6, 2005.

Audie Leon Murphy, 1934 - 1971.

Capt. Eddie Rickenbacker, October 8, 1890 - July 27, 1973, Founder of Eastern Airlines.

Andrew Jackson, March 15, 1767 - June 8, 1845,
1st Governor of Florida, 7th President of US.

Church where Susan Hayword filmed "I'd Climb the Highest Mountain".

Johnny Cash, February 26, 1932 - September 12, 2003
and June Carter Cash, June 23, 1929 - May 15, 2003.

PICKING A FINAL
RESTING PLACE

WOULD YOU LIKE HOT SAUCE ON YOUR TACO?

It is sad, but prejudice in the deep South rears its ugly head even after death. I was walking the cemetery with Mrs. Martin who was looking for a proper resting place for her husband.

"I don't want him buried next to any Negroes or Mexicans." Mrs. Martin said firmly. "Mr. Martin was very adamant about not associating with Blacks or Mexicans in his life."

"Mrs. Martin, you can't always tell by the name on the headstone what the nationality is."

"Can't you look it up in the office?"

"I could but I won't. That's private information." I always tried to console the grieving widow, but Mrs. Martin was making it tough.

"Well, then we'll just look for some really American names. Real Americans wouldn't associate with them either." She determined. What she didn't realize was that Mexicans were more real Americans than American settlers, having been on the American continent long before we were. We found some names like Smith and Jones and that made Mrs. Martin happy.

After the burial, and a goodly amount of time had elapsed, I got curious. I was checking the files because we had a burial near by Mr. Martin's grave, and I noticed that Mr. Martin was buried next to a Mexican lady married to a John Smith. I hope Mr. Martin likes Tacos in his afterlife, because that's what he's probably being served!

THE OFFICER'S CLUB

I made pre-arrangements for burial with the Barton family and we went out to the cemetery to pick out their spaces.

"I'm a retired colonel." Mr. Barton began as we walked through the Veteran's Garden. "I don't want to be buried next to any enlisted men. I didn't associate with them when I was on active duty, and I don't want to associate with them now. And, I don't plan to associate with them after death." Mr. Barton looked at me, and I think he expected me to salute.

"Well," I started. "It might be kind of hard to find a space between two officers. We would have to do a really lengthy search of headstones."

"It's a pretty day. I've got the time. Shall we get started?" The colonel gave his command. We searched the better part of the afternoon before we found a space between two officers. Colonel Barton was happy, so we went to the office and finalized the paperwork.

A few years later, he died. After his burial, Mrs. Barton said she was also a veteran and gave me her DD214 form for the file. DD214's are needed to apply for Veterans benefits and their flag on the grave. I read on the DD214 that she had served as a sergeant in the Army.

I got so mad at the deceased Colonel Barton because he refused to be buried next to an enlisted person, yet, he'd been sleeping with one for years! I even thought about digging him up, and moving him between two enlisted people, but then I figured being buried next to his wife was punishment enough.

SꙈꞢꞢꝌꙈꞤD SꝌꙈꞤD

I had a friend named Mark that lost his fourteen year old son in a motorcycle accident. He came to the cemetery to pick out a space for his son.

"Lee," he said as we walked the grounds. "Greg was so full of life. I don't want him buried next to any grumpy old people."

"Mark," I tried to explain. "The cemetery's full of old people. We don't have that many young people that die. How about Baby Land?" I offered as we entered the garden guarded by two baby angels.

"No, that would insult him. He wouldn't want to be seen as a baby."

His father pondered. "He was hip. He was cool. He was a ' teen-ager. His music would drive the old people out of their caskets and into the office to complain."

"Mark, I'll do you a favor. I have some space between the hedge and the road that is only big enough for one grave. We'll put Greg there and he can play his music as loud as he wants." Mark shook my hand in agreement and slapped me on the back. He was very happy his son was going to have private quarters! I would do almost anything to help family members get through their grief and into a better space as Mark obviously became.

TꞪꞒ WIꞤꞤIꞤꞖ BID

I met with two couples from Ohio, The Clifford's and the Davis's, that have been friends for years. They followed each other to Florida and did everything together including their pre-arrangements for burial. We walked through the cemetery to pick out their spaces.

"We must be end to end like we are at a card table." Began Mrs. Clifford.

"Quite right, dear." Said Mrs. Davis. "We've played cards two or three times a week for years, and we do want the same seats we've always had." We stopped in front of four vacant spaces, two across from two.

"In this garden," I persuaded, "You are buried the way you are married. That would put you across from each other- male, female, male, female."

"Lee, you're a genius!" Mr. Clifford yelled, while slapping Mr. Davis on the back.

"Only one thing," I warned in a dead serious tone. "No loud noises or drunken parties. People are at rest, here."

"Oh Lee, you're no fun." Mrs. Clifford pouted.

"He won't be able to hear us at the office. And he does go home at night." Mrs. Davis chimed in. We had a good laugh and they bought all four spaces!

I WANT TO RENT A ROOM WITH A VIEW

I felt so sorry for this one guy. His grief was driving him bananas. This gentleman came to the cemetery every day to visit his wife in the Mausoleum. He kept telling me he couldn't go on without her, and we would have to escort him out of the cemetery after hours. I really felt for him.

"Lee, I can't write a check. I don't have an idea about anything. Mary used to do all that."

"You'll learn, John." I comforted. "Life goes on."

"Lee, I'll give you my life's savings if you put me in the crypt with her." John offered. "At least she could tell me how to do stuff."

"John, you know that's not possible." After that I really kept an eye on him. I didn't want to find him dead up there just to get the room with the view. Grief can make people crazy, but passing through grief can make people stronger. John would be strong again.

CROSSING THE GARDEN

Once I had a Jewish burial in Veterans Garden. We had a Jewish Veteran coming into the cemetery for burial by a local funeral home. I met the funeral at the gate and was escorting them to the gravesite. As I was escorting the funeral in, I noticed in my rear view mirror that the procession had stopped. I got out of the car and went back to see what was wrong.

The funeral director and I had forgotten that the Veterans Garden featured a rather large cross. The veteran's mother was highly upset that her son was going to be buried by the cross.

"Tell you, what I'll do." I told the funeral director. "Let's drive the procession around the cemetery real slow, and I'll have my maintenance crew set up another tent, lowering device and chairs in the Garden of David. It's a new garden I just opened up for deceased members of the Jewish faith."

"Sounds great." He said. We went around the cemetery at a snail's pace. In fact, I think we went around twice. The people in the procession probably wondered what was going on, but everybody was happy when we got to the Garden of David. The family was very happy with me, and that's all that counted.

UNTIL DEATH DO US PART

A Catholic lady married to a Jew came in to make arrangements for her husband's burial. She really didn't seem to be the mourning widow type, but each person handles her grief in her own way.

"Would you like to reserve or buy the space next to him for your burial?" I asked. "You want it to be available when you need it."

"I had to sleep with him for thirty years but I don't have to spend an eternity with him." She stated adamantly. So for herself, she purchased a space in the Garden of Prophecy, which is our Catholic Garden.

Along the same lines, I had an Avenue of Flags that we established for families to remember their family members on their birthdates. We would raise the flag each day and their names would be on the plaque at the base of the flagpole. One day, I was interviewing this lady for arrangements for her husband's burial.

"I want my husband's flag raised each year on October 31st." She demanded.

"Oh, was he born on Halloween?" I asked with interest.

"No, but he was such a horror to live with, I want it raised on Halloween!"

I guess we really don't know how our spouses feel about us until after we're gone. I hope my wife has nice things to say about me after I die!

FLOWERS FOR
?????????????????

A ROSE IS A ROSE IS A WILTED ROSE

One day, after a week in the hot sun, we had just cleared the flowers off the grave of Mr. Tabs, when Mrs. Tabs came in.

"Good Morning, Mrs. Tabs. What can I do for you?"

"There are no flowers on my husband's grave. What happened to them?" She asked. "Those flowers were beautiful the last time I was here. I wanted them back. I was going to take them home."

"Mrs. Tabs, you must have realized they wouldn't last forever. Only diamonds last forever." I joked.

"The price that was paid for those flowers was forever, and I want them back."

Ordinarily, we wouldn't have been able to accommodate a request like that because the flowers would have been destroyed or recycled, but we had just taken them off the grave. So, we went down to the shed, and my men helped load Mrs. Tabs' wilted and shedding flowers into her station wagon. She drove off happy with her compost.

You would think after a week or two, people would know their flowers wouldn't last, but you'd be amazed at the number of people who come in wanting their flowers back. The smart ones use artificial flowers, or figure out that 95 degree heat and fresh flowers don't mix.

NO FLOWERS FROM YOU, THANK YOU

Another time a young widow came to me in tears.

"Whatever is the matter, Mrs. Softer?" I asked seeing her distress.

"Oh Mr. Downs. Whenever I put flowers on my husband's grave, the Captain throws them away."

"Who's the Captain?"

"That's my father-in-law. He says that he paid for the grave marker and I can't put flowers there. He never did like me very much."

"That's awful, Mrs. Softer." The woman was on her second handkerchief. "I'll talk to him. You go home and get some rest now."

She looked up through her tears and said, "Oh thank you, Mr. Downs." I waited for her to leave, found her father-in-law's number and picked up the phone.

"Hello, Mr. Softer?"

"That's Captain Softer. Retired United States Navy. Who is this?"

"I'm Lee Downs, owner of the cemetery where your son is buried. I just saw your daughter-in-law, and she says you won't let her put flowers on your son's grave."

"That's Maggie. I hate that woman. She's been divorced three times. How do I know my son wasn't going to be number four?"

"She must have loved him very much or she wouldn't want to keep flowers on his grave."

"Guilty conscience, probably. But even if she did love him, flowers on his grave every week are too much fluff."

"Well, how about on his birthday, Christmas, and special occasions?"

"O.K., I guess I can live with that." The Captain relented.

"Thank you, sir."

I called Maggie and gave her the good news, and the next time she put flowers on her husband's grave, I found a rose on my desk. Sweet kid.

WHO SENT THESE?

Some of the traditions of the different ethnic groups regarding flowers are very interesting. Mr. King, a black funeral home director, was doing a ceremony during a wake in my chapel. I slipped in the back and watched. He picked up the first basket of flowers and faced the congregation.

"This lovely arrangement of roses and baby's breath is from the Martin family. Mary would have loved them very much." He set down that basket and picked up the next.

"Here, we have a lovely arrangement of yellow, Gerber daisies and wildflowers from Mr. and Mrs. Smith. Mary would have loved the colors." He set that one down and picked up the next. He picked up every basket in the room, described it, and told who they were from. If it were me, I wouldn't send something cheap because the whole room would know about it. The ceremony is a nice custom though, and I am sure it gives the family a lot of comfort.

Another nice touch is when I see family members and friends file by an open grave and drop flowers on the casket. Sometimes, they drop flowers in the casket after the service. Flowers are a sign of new life in the afterlife with their Maker. In the mist of tragedy, there is always hope.

GRANDMAS WITH FLOWER POWER

One of the hardest jobs in the cemetery business is keeping flowers on the graves. I could stand at my window in my office that overlooked the whole cemetery, and watch elderly people remove flowers from someone else's grave, and put them on their own loved one's grave. People spend a lot of money on flowers and get understandably upset when something happens to them.

I had one little, old lady, Mrs. Mable, who was infamous for stealing flowers. I was looking out my office window one day when I saw her stealing flowers off of somebody's grave. I hurried out to confront her.

"Mrs. Mable, you know those don't belong to you." She was standing over Mr. Allen's grave, holding a basket of flowers when I knew her husband's grave was in the next row. I caught her red-handed.

"These flowers are getting too much sun here. I was just moving them to protect them." She rationalized.

"Put them back, Mrs. Mable." I said sternly.

"Alright, Lee. You caught me." Mrs. Mable sighed. "But you know I'm on a fixed income. I can't afford flowers. How about I put half back and I keep half?"

"Put them back, Mrs. Mable." I stood my ground. The little, old lady put them back, and I escorted her out of the cemetery. There's no point in calling the police. I'm not going to put somebody's grandmother or great-grandmother in jail. I just keep my eyes open for grandmas who think they have flower power.

CEMETERY CRITTERS

ARMADILLOS, ONE~ ME, ZERO

While I was living in the cemetery, I noticed Armadillos doing damage to our grounds. I was constantly at war with them, trying to catch them. Shooting them with my 22 wasn't any good because my bullets just bounced off their armored shells.

One night, I had been out in my brand new Lincoln Mark 7, and had had a few drinks. Coming into the cemetery about midnight, I saw one of the Armadillos crossing the entrance drive. He stopped in the middle, looked up and smiled at me, and continued on his way.

I gave chase in my new luxury car. He led me down the road right into our drain path causing much damage to the front of my car. My car had to be pulled out, and I glanced on the shoulder of the road when the truck got there. There sat the Armadillo, and if I didn't know better, I swear he was laughing at me.

BIRDS OF A FEATHER

When I was chairman of the CRA (Community Redevelopment Association), we were responsible for getting Lee Boulevard made into six lanes. At one of our meetings, there was a wet-behind-the-ears, college grad that challenged me as to why I wanted the road widened.

"Mr. Downs," The kid stood at the mike accusing. "Widening the road would damage the habitat of the red-headed cockades and result in loss of life."

"I've never heard of the red headed cockade but I assume it's a bird." I clarified.

"Yes, it is."

"Well, I have a funeral home on Lee Boulevard, and I've never buried a red-headed cockade, but I have buried quite a few people that were killed on Lee Boulevard." The kid shut up and sat down.

SURPRISE! SURPRISE! SURPRISE!

Snakes caused a lot of funny business in the cemetery. I never had any use for snakes and neither did my business partner. Snakes caused us nothing but trouble.

One day, I heard screaming coming from my outdoor Chapel Mausoleum. We had added a couple of rest rooms by the chapel for the convenience of visitors. The screaming was coming from the Ladies Room.

I rushed around the corner to see what the problem was. An elderly lady was running out of the bathroom. I never saw someone so old move so fast.

"A snake! A snake!" She screamed. "I was about to sit down on the bowl, when I happened to glance down and see the snake leering up at me from inside the toilet!" She cried breathlessly. "I was so upset, I even left my walker in the Ladies Room."

I'm glad she didn't sit down. I would have had trouble explaining a snakebite on the tush to an ambulance driver. I calmed her down, and called my maintenance man. He removed the snake and retrieved her walker from the Ladies

Room. After a cup of coffee at the office and two aspirin, the lady was good to go. But she promised never to use my toilet, again!

THE DEVIL AND REVEREND JONES

Another time, we had a funeral service led by Reverend Jones in the chapel. Now, Reverend Jones was a real fire and brimstone preacher. My partner and I were in the back by the aisle.

"The devil comes in many forms." Reverend Jones preached. "Our dear departed Tony recognized the devil in lust, greed, hatred, and in many other forms. He avoided the devil with a passion, and led a good life. Will we avoid the devil?"

I noticed my partner gradually backing up towards the door with a look of fear on his face. I looked down and there was a rattlesnake crawling towards us. Here was the devil in person, I thought. I got a maintenance man with a pole that had a rope noose wrapped around it, to quietly enter and remove the snake from the back of the chapel without ever disturbing the service. The only one who could see what was going on was Reverend Jones, and he didn't let on a thing. I think he was too scared to.

THERE'S NO CHARM IN SNAKE CHARMERS

Perhaps, the weirdest snake story involved a local minister. Reverend Martin had a restaurant in town and specialized in country food. The name of the restaurant was Rev. Martin's Country Kitchen and all his employees were church members. I loved to eat there. I never inquired about his beliefs until the day his wife was to be buried at my cemetery.

He informed me that he had containers of snakes that he used for his services and that I might want to help him with his snakes, today. I immediately told him of my lack of love for the crawly monsters. Needless to say, I didn't even watch the service.

I never would have guessed that the restaurant people where I ate were snake worshippers. I never ate there again. I'm not superstitious or anything, but after we buried his wife, her grave kept sinking in, and we had to continually re-sod it. Pretty spooky, huh?

CREMATIONS

JACK AND JILL BROWN

Jack and Jill Brown were good friends of mine who were very realistic about their own deaths, and found humor in the mist of tragedy. Jill always talked with her arms waving.

"Jill, I'm going to put you In the casket with your arms raised, so people will know it's you." I teased.

"Well, make sure you shave my arm pits, first." She shot back. "I don't want people thinking I'm not well-groomed."

She also wanted to be buried in a Plexiglas casket so people could see her whole body while sitting in the chapel.

"If you pay a lot for a funeral dress, people should be able to see it!" In addition, Jill wanted her three urns of dog pets buried with her in the casket.

The day Jill died, she called my wife, Fran, and asked her to come over and help her bathe because she was going to die. She told Fran she could wash her own tush, thank you, but Fran could help with the rest.

Jill was quite a character. Her husband, Jack, must have thought so too, because the next day, I found him dead in the bathroom. He just gave up and laid down on the bathroom floor and died. So, I cremated him and buried Jack and Jill and the three dogs in the same casket. Now there's a family that stayed together till the end.

JOAN AND RICHARD

When you live in a small town like Lehigh Acres, you end up selling pre-need (advanced funeral arrangements to your friends. I had known Richard and Joan for some years. Joan was a well-known local restaurant hostess and a hostess at a local dinner theater. She had a reputation for always kidding everyone. My pre-need session with Richard and Joan was hilarious.

"What are your needs and desires when you pass, Joan?" I asked in all sincerity.

"What do I need? I need a naked picture of Tom Selleck in the lid of my casket, so we'll be face to face when the lid is closed. Eternity is a long time."

"Joan," I laughed. "It's going to be kind of hard to get Tom's naked picture, but I'll be glad to put one of me in the lid."

"No thank you, Lee. Like I said, eternity is a long time."

"Gee, thanks."

Richard, who had been sitting there quietly through all this decided he was not going to be outdone.

"When I die, I want to be cremated. Mix my ashes in a bucket of white paint and paint our bedroom ceiling with it. If she decides to get a new lover, I'm going to flake all over her!"

I DON'T WANT A BURNT OFFERING

I had a habit of donating a free space in the cemetery for parties or benefit auctions and raffles. After I opened up the crematory, I even offered free cremations. One night, at a Shrine function, they were looking for door prizes, and I offered a free cremation. I wrote it on the back of a business card.

The lady that won it, was only a few tables away from me. She got up, and I could tell she had had one too many. She started yelling at me.

"I don't want to die! And I don't want to be cremated!" She let the whole room know.

"You don't have to die, now." I soothed. "You can use it later, or use it for someone in your family."

"I don't want to be toast. And I don't want anybody in my family to be toast." She sat back down, but she wasn't too happy. I did notice she slipped the business card in her purse.

About three days later, a relative of hers died in La Belle, and she called me up to use the free cremation. I had to restrain myself from saying anything, but I honored the free cremation. Fear of paying a bill was greater than her fear of cremation!

I'LL GIVE YOU A FREE CREMATION

Tom Willard was a pervert who preyed on and murdered young boys. He was finally electrocuted. He had just been arrested in Pine Island, Florida for molesting and murdering a nine year-old boy. At that time, my son was nine years old. I felt complete hatred for this guy.

While in jail, he complained that he only had a black and white T.V. to watch, and the Sheriff's department wouldn't do anything for his acne. I wrote a letter to the editor of the newspaper. I said there were a lot of good people out there working for a living who only had black and white T.V. sets.

I also told the newspaper that I had a brand new crematory and would be glad to cremate his acne off for free. In fact, I would be glad to cremate him for free- while he was still alive!

FROM ASHES SPRING ROSES

In my garden of Reflection I had a pond (the reflecting pond) and around it, I planted rose bushes. So being the genius I am, I decided to use it as a cremation garden. The calcium in cremains is a good fertilizer for roses.

Families would elect to sprinkle their loved ones ashes in the Rose Garden, and have a small bronze plate on the brick wall around the pond to remember their loved one by. After several years, I had the healthiest, prettiest roses in town!

MOM WAS A GEM

Another choice I gave to the families that wanted to keep something of their loved ones with them was jewelry. We had necklaces, rings, bracelets, barrettes , and pendants that would hold a small amount of ashes. There is nothing like having Mom in a ring to always remember her by.

FAMILIES THAT SHARE

We had remembrance urns for family members to share mom and dad's cremains. They could be set on a knick-knack shelf or cabinet and the casual observer wouldn't know what it contained. I had one family with five children and they didn't want dad's ashes thrown away, so I sold them five cremenbrance urns to keep dad with all of them. One thing about cremains- there's always enough to go around no matter how big the family is!

WHISKEY CREEK

One of the funniest funerals I did was burying a local fisherman at sea. When he died, the wife had me cremate him and put his cremains in a Jack Daniels bottle.

We set sail on a bright, sunny morning and had our service on the Gulf of Mexico. I poured the ashes into the sea with the bottle following shortly after. On the way back to port, I asked the wife why she wanted his cremains in a Jack Daniels bottle.

"I always told him he was going to crawl into a Jack Daniels bottle and die." She stated matter of factly. "Well, he finally did it." She offered me a shot and we drank in his memory.

BEVERLY AND MR. JONES

Sometimes, the U.S. mail delivers more than dead letters as was the case with Beverly, Jim Fortana's secretary at the Lehigh Corporation. Her P.O. Box number was 968 and mine was 568.

"Hi Lee, I think the post office sent something of yours to my P.O. box. I have a small box on my desk and it's leaking."

"Where's it from?" I asked rather casually.

"I don't know. Let me look at the label." There was a pause on the phone. "Oh, my God!" She gasped. "It's from a crematory!"

"Be careful with that box. That's Mr. Jones and it's not leaking- that's ashes."

"You get your ass over here right now and get this thing off my desk!" Beverly was so upset, I thought I would have a little bit of fun with her.

"Alright, Beverly. I'll be right over. But don't mess with those ashes. It might be a leg or an arm or something." I can't repeat all the things she called me, but I did go over right away and get those ashes off her desk and bury Mr. Jones.

EMPLOYEES

DOUG SWIFT

Doug Swift was my sales manager. He was an insurance salesman in Ohio and got tired of the ice and the snow. He packed his golf clubs and came to Florida. He told his wife and kids he would send for them when he got a job. I hired him and he was with me for eight years. He was good at selling and made good money.

There was just one little problem with Doug. He was scared of the cemetery and would not come on the grounds after dark. He wouldn't meet customers in the cemetery if they wanted to come after work to talk to him.

We had a golf cart that we used to take perspective customers around in for tours of the cemetery. I made a rule that the last one to use the cart had to take it to the shed and put the charger on it for the evening. The shed also housed the crematory. Doug would pay other employees, even the secretaries, to take the golf cart to the shed and plug it in for him because he didn't want to see the crematory.

Now, Bruno was my crematory operator. He had thick, dark eyebrows and a devilish smile. The shirts he wore were always too small and his fat, hairy belly hung out. Bruno's sole purpose in life was to aggravate Doug or so it seemed, anyway.

One day, Doug had an appointment in North Fort Myers. A funeral home there called me and said that they had stillborn twins to cremate. I told them I would send my salesman over to pick them up since he was going to be in the area. I asked them to please not to tell him what was in the box. I ask them just to put the box in the truck and to tell him it was mail for me. The funeral home did as I requested.

When Doug got back to the cemetery, Bruno met him at his car.

"Did you bring the babies?" Bruno asked.

"What babies? What are you talking about? I just have some mail for Lee." Doug answered defensively.

"Oh no, buddy. You're carrying two dead babies. What me to open the box and show you?"

At that moment, Doug ran away from his car. He came into my office.

"Why didn't you tell me what you wanted me to pick up?"

"Because you wouldn't have picked them up."

"You're right. I wouldn't have. Now, I'm going to have nightmares all night."

"You'll live."

Another day, I was standing at the door of my office talking to Doug and Bruno came up. I appreciate the fact that the crematory operator works in the heat of the day. His shirt was completely unbuttoned and his big hairy belly was in full view.

"Lee, we've got a problem." Bruno started.

"What is it?" I asked concerned.

"It's the crematory."

"What's wrong?"

"It's not getting hot enough." At that moment Bruno pulled out from behind his back this big, bloody, leg of lamb and bit into it right in front of Doug's face. We all laughed but Doug turned white and slid down from the door to the floor. With a little smelling salts, he came to and Bruno was gone, retreating to attack another day. After eight years you would have thought that Doug would have gotten used to the profession, but each day was a challenge for him. At least, his work stayed interesting!

Two For The Road

The strange wishes of funeral arrangements are not limited to the general public but also extended to my employees. Mary was a secretary and part time sales agent for me. She was very proud of her endowment and swore that everyone wanted to see them. We were talking one day in the office and she expressed her desire.

"Hey, Lee. Do we have to cover up these puppies with a dress when I die?" Mary ran a hand over her chest. "I mean everyone's enjoyed looking at them when I'm alive, why not after I'm dead?"

"Mary, for you we will bury you naked and in a Plexiglas casket so everybody can see them after you're gone." I was only joking but Mary said, "Oh thank you Lee. I can rest in peace now." Vanity thy name is woman!

SOME OF MY FRIENDS

THE HIP BONE'S CONNECTED TO THE LEG BONE

I had a good friend named Jim Fortana. Now, Jim is the epitome of Italian and doesn't believe he is ever going to die nor did he like to talk about death. What was so funny was that he was my senior vice president of the cemetery in Lehigh Acres, Florida. He would only ask me how things were going at the cemetery and very rarely would he come out to see the cemetery or the crematory.

I used to take surgical steel prosthetic devices after cremation and shine them up and present them to friends as letter openers. Well, one day, I took a letter opener to Jim.

"What's this?" He took it in his hand and glanced at it.

"It's a letter opener."

"Thanks, Lee. I can always use a letter opener.

"Yea, it was an artificial hip joint from one of my bodies. They're sharp as razors."

Jim immediately dropped it and started yelling at me in Italian. I took that to mean it was time for me to leave. Funny thing about that letter opener. I don't think he ever used it.

TO DIE OR NOT TO DIE...
THAT IS THE QUESTION

I'll never be able to figure out my friend, Jim Fortana. When he was senior vice president of the Lehigh Corporation, I offered him many opportunities to purchase crypts at cost and funeral arrangements at a big discount, and he always gave me the same answer.

"I'm not ready, and nothing is going to happen to me." He use to think he was immortal.

Well, since I've retired, (and he's gotten a little older), he has decided that death may well be a possibility. Jim made his arrangements with me, and I thought that would be the end of it.

Now, he's become a man obsessed, and is always calling me to keep everything updated. I travel a lot in my retirement, and am not always available for him. Recently, he called me up and said, "Honest to God, Lee... if I die and you're not here, I'll never speak to you again!"

IT'S ALL IN THE NUMBERS

When I was ready to leave the cemetery in Lehigh Acres, my phone number was 369-2602. The local Elks Lodge was #2602, and they wanted my phone number so it would be easy for their members to remember. I agreed to give it to them. One day, Arnie, an Elks Lodge officer called me.

"Hi, Lee. This is Arnie from the Elks."

" Hi, Arnie. How are you?"

"I'm O.K. But that phone number you gave us is something else."

"Oh?"

"Yea, you wouldn't believe the phone calls we get to pick up dead bodies, schedule funerals, and other stuff."

"Sorry about that, Arnie. I guess I should have told you that phone number was on thousands of business cards and cemetery literature that was passed out over the twenty years I worked there."

"Well," said Arnie. "The only kind of stiffs we deal with here are the working kind. I'm going to send everybody else your way."

"No problem Arnie. I can direct them to the right place." And the right place was not the Elks Lodge!

RINGING IN THE THIEVES

I had a policy at the crematory that if the family wanted their loved ones cremated with their jewelry that we would tape the jewelry to the inside lid of the urn after cremation, just in case the family ever came back and wanted the jewelry. I'm not a jeweler, and I don't know a $2.00 Avon ring from a $10,000 diamond. It looks all the same to me.

Well, one day, Joe, a fellow Shriner friend of mine came in. His wife had been cremated for over five years.

"Hi, Joe. What can I do for you?" I greeted.

"Well, yesterday was my anniversary. I got to thinking about the wife. You know, when I bought her her diamond, she never took it off her finger, not even when she was doing dishes."

"She must have loved it very much."

"Yea, she did. If it's not too much trouble, I'd like to see it. It reminds me of her."

"Sure thing, Joe. We'll go down there right now." We began our walk to the niche.

"You know, I paid a fortune for that ring... 75 hundred dollars. But to see the joy on her face when I put it on her finger was worth every penny."

Suddenly, I started worrying if the crew had done as they were instructed and taped the ring to the lid. My people were as honest as the day was long, but to someone who knew something about jewelry, it would be a big temptation.

"Well, here we are." I stood in front of the niche and said a silent prayer. With fear and trepidation, I opened the Niche and the Urn, and sure enough, the ring was there. Joe picked it up, looked at it, and handed it back to me. Joe was satisfied, and I taped it back to the lid of the urn. Boy, was I relieved it was there as promised! No thieves had gotten to the ring, and closed up in the urn and locked in the niche, no one probably ever would.

LET ME MAKE YOU AN OFFER YOU CAN'T REFUSE

I actually had two offers for big bucks I wouldn't touch with a ten foot pole. In the seventies, there was a lot of drug smuggling in South Florida. My cemetery was in the boondocks outside the Everglades. We were in the path of drug smugglers going from Fort Myers and La Belle to Miami and other points.

One of our local funeral directors who I thought I was pretty good friends with came to see me one day.

"Hi Tony, come on in the office." I welcomed. "What brings you to this neck of the woods?"

"Lee, can we talk in private?"

"We are in private." Tony seemed nervous.

"I have friends in high places. They've authorized me to offer you ten grand in cash for the key to your crematory."

I gave a low whistle. Then, I started thinking what these "friends" wanted my crematory for. The crematory could dispose of evidence. Or someone that was in the way. I didn't want to get involved because first of all, they might be doing something illegal, and secondly, I might end up as that someone in the way!

"No thanks, Tony. I think you better go." I showed him the door. "And don't come back."

"O.K., but it's your loss."

It wasn't too long after that, I heard Tony ended up in jail.

The second offer for big bucks I could and did refuse, came when these two guys approached me to buy my Winnebago. I had a Winnebago motor home the wife and I use to travel in. These two guys wanted to buy it on the spot, and offered me twenty grand for it.

I admit, it was tempting. But I knew it wasn't worth half that much. I got suspicious and drove away. Winnebagos and small motor homes were used to transport drugs because they were inconspicuous. I'm really glad I didn't take any of that money. In the months that followed, one of our local sheriffs went to jail for covering for drug runners, and one of the richest men in the area went to jail for letting drug runners use his property. I'll keep my day job, thank you.

A CASE OF MISTAKEN IDENTITY

John Jones, one of the friends that stood up for me at my wedding, was a retired, New York Cop. He was always very jovial- never met a person he didn't like- always laughing and always telling jokes.

His mother was named, "Mary." There was another man in town whose name was also John Jones and his wife was named, "Mary." Well, my friend's mother died and we ran the obituary in the paper saying the services would be Friday evening at such and such a time. Everybody come by for the visitation.

John was standing at the door with tears in his eyes, greeting people. I was standing in the lobby like I always do. I showed people where the register book was and had them sign in. In walks this gentleman, and signs the book for Mary Jones. He walks up to the casket, and looks down at Mary.

"That's not Mary Jones!" he shouted. "I've known Mary Jones for thirty years. And that's not Mary Jones!"

John wiped his wet eyes, and went over to talk to the man. "That is too, Mary Jones. That's my mother, Mary."

"No, no." said the man. "I've known Mary and her husband for years. And that's not Mary Jones." Soft chuckles could be heard throughout the room.

It took just a second for my friend to get on his game. "Well, maybe next time." John laughed. The man indignantly turned on his heel, walked out of the room, and entered the lobby. He went to the register book and erased his name. He ran out the back door followed by a roomful of laughter.

VINNIE AND THE DEAD BODY

When I first opened up the crematory at the cemetery, I had a cooler where we stored bodies in downtown Fort Myers. Funeral homes around the area that used my crematory, also dropped bodies off at the cooler. Funeral directors would call me to pick up bodies from the cooler for cremation. Someone would call and say "John Smith" or whoever, was ready for cremation the next day, and I would go down and pick up the paperwork, do the cremation, and return the cremains to the funeral home.

I had a very, good friend, Vinnie, who was retired Navy. He spent thirty years as a submarine commander and was tattooed from his neck to his ankles. I figured this had to be the toughest cookie I ever met.

We used to go to the Shriner's Club on Thursday nights. We would have our meetings, and afterwards we would play a little poker and have a couple of drinks. Now, Vinnie didn't like to drink and drive. So, he would ride home with me in my hearse. Being superstitious, he didn't like to talk about death, or see death, or know anything about death. I always had to take the hearse to the club, in case I had to pick up a body for cremation. Consequently, when we would drive to the club and back, in the hearse, if there was a box in the back, Vinnie would not even look that way but keep his eyes straight ahead.

One night, Vinnie's wife was out of town, and we were coming home about midnight. I had to stop by the cooler and pick up a body for cremation. After backing up to the door, I went about the business of loading the body into a cremation container. I happened to look up, and here's my friend. He tweaked the toes of the body I was picking up.

"What the hell are you doing?" I asked.

"I just wanted to touch one. You know I've never been around dead people." Vinnie explained.

"O.K., you touched one. Get back in the hearse and let's go home." I said in a tired voice. I dropped Vinnie off, and went home and fell into a deep sleep. About three o'clock in the morning, the phone rang. It was Vinnie and he was shouting.

"You son of a gun! You S.O.B.! You let me touch that dead body!"

"I didn't let you touch that dead body. You did that on your own."

"I can't sleep. You never should have let me in there. Helen's out of town, and I have to sleep by myself and have bad dreams."

And this was the toughest cookie I ever met. That was the last time he ever rode in my hearse, barring one instance. When the guys at the club heard about this night, we decided to play a little joke on Vinnie. I put an empty box in the back of my hearse which was actually a converted station wagon.

Vinnie and I went to the club. The boys and I had a plan. One of our Shriners who was a little bit of a mischievous jokester decided he would get into the box, and when I was driving my friend home, he was going to reach out of the box and tap Vinnie on the shoulder. We got quite a few laughs out of this while we were planning it. But in the end, I wouldn't let the guys do it.

I was afraid Vinnie would die of fright. As it turned out, a few weeks later, Vinnie had a heart attack, so I know he would have had one if we had carried out our plan. It wouldn't have been very much fun to have to have given him mouth to mouth resuscitation. He was kind of ugly.

DRIVE-THRU FUNERAL

harry, a good friend of mine, was the local electrician and ex-deputy. I always thought he was a pretty tough guy until he lost his mother. He came to the funeral home and sat out front blowing the horn. I went to see what the problem was.

"What's the problem, Harry?"

"Mom passed, and I need to make arrangements for her funeral."

"I'm sorry, Harry. Come inside and we'll fill out the paperwork."

"Nothing doing. You bring the paperwork out here." He rested on his steering wheel.

I thought to myself, this isn't a drive-thru bank or McDonald's or Hardee's, but far be it for me to question the bereaved. So, I got a clipboard and stood by his car and filled out the paperwork.

"Now, Harry, I need to know for the death certificate what your mother's mother's name was."

"Grandma."

I could see I was getting nowhere with Harry, so I sent him on his way, and got the information I needed from his wife. When they had the service for his mother, he wouldn't even come in. He just sat out in his car in the parking lot. He died a few years later, and I thought this time he has to come into the funeral home because I don't do drive-thru wakes and funerals.

STRANGE REQUESTS

ONE UP ON MOM

Even my ghost writer, Kathleen, made it into my book when she told me of her strange request in her own words:

After my husband divorced me and I had moved in with my mother in Florida, she began to worry about who was going to bury me. I had no husband, no children, and being the youngest in the family would probably outlive everybody else.

She had already made all the pre-arrangements for her funeral, and convinced me to buy a pre-need package. I bought a cemetery plot not far from my parents. Since my mother had had such a hard life, she wanted the words, "I tried." Inscribed on her tombstone.

I thought about visitors to the graveyard, seeing her grave and then a few feet down, seeing my grave. I paid 1600 dollars to have "Number Two Tried Harder" inscribed on my headstone. I always had to be one up on mom.

THE FAMILY JEWELS

I had a young lady, Miss Scott, come to the funeral home one day with an unusual request.

"Mr. Downs, I want you to disinter my grandmother."

"Whatever for?" I asked horrified.

"My mother recently died, and left all grandmother's jewelry to me."

"That's a good thing, isn't it?" I ventured.

"No, not really. When I was a little girl, I was constantly trying on grandmother's jewelry, and the old bat kept saying, 'don't touch that! Take that off!' So now, I can't wear any of it because I keep hearing her voice." Miss Scott explained. "I want her jewelry buried with her. Then, I know she'll be at peace."

"Don't you think she's already at rest?" I asked. "Besides disinterring her would be expensive and would require a new vault."

"I don't care. I want to get rid of the jewelry." She said it like a jewel thief with hot merchandise.

We did as she wished, and placed the jewelry with the grandmother. There is no word, yet, on whether her mother let her play with her jewelry. I wouldn't have to dig mom up, too.

WHEN IRISH EYES ARE DRINKING

I had a very strict, Irish Catholic family that wanted to stay with their dear ole dad after the wake. They wanted to spend the night in the chapel with him like they did in the homeland.

"Please, Mr. Downs." The eldest son pleaded. "We believe that death is a celebration because our loved one is with the Lord. Why, at me grandfather's wake, we even stood the corpse up in the corner, and me grandmother danced the jig with him."

"There will be none of that here." I cautioned. They were so insistent, I finally said O.K. However, I wasn't going to spend the night with them. "Just don't go in or out of the building because I am leaving the alarm on."

"Sure thing, Mr. Downs."

The next day, the room was filled with empty, Irish whiskey bottles. There was even one or two full bottles in the casket for dear ole dad to take with him. What I don't understand, is they couldn't go out because the alarm was on. How did they get all that whiskey in the funeral home unless they had it hidden on their person under their suits during the wake? Now I know why Irish eyes smile.

CAUGHT WITH HIS PANTS UP

I always try to explain to families things about burial and cremation. Sometimes, I offer them more than they really want to know, and sometimes, without realizing it, I don't give them enough information.

One day, at a funeral for a young man, this lady came up and spoke to me. "Please don't laugh, but y'all buried my son nine years ago, and I've always wondered if he had his pants on. "

"Of course, he had his pants on," I said. "What would we do with a pair of trousers?" I joked. Then, I realized she was serious. "Yes, he had his pants on, and his boxer shorts, too. " I comforted. "Why did you wait so long to ask?"

"I was afraid to ask. I thought you might think I was crazy."

"A lot of people wonder about shoes, socks, underwear, etc., so don't be afraid to ask." I explained.

"Thanks. I paid a bundle for those Haggers trousers for his birthday, and I wanted to make sure he got good use out of them!"

YES, WE HAVE SOME BANANNAS

Another time, our funeral director had made arrangements with a family to bury old dad, who must have been quite a jokester. After the family left, the daughter came back to talk to me.

"Mr. Downs," she asked. "I have a strange request."

"What is it, dear?" In this business, I've heard it all, so I didn't think I'd be surprised.

She pushed a bag towards me. "Could you put on these under shorts we got him for Father's Day and not tell anyone?"

"Of course, dear. That's not a strange request. That's sentimental."

"Oh, thank you!" she beamed.

Later that night, the undertaker called me into the preparation room to show me the shorts. He turned off the lights and the shorts had bananas on them that glowed in the dark! We had a good laugh, and figured old dad had one, too!

LIFE'S A BEACH

I have done a lot of unusual funerals before, but this one took the cake. Miss Dee, barely more than a teen-ager, came in to make arrangements for her young mother who had died in her forties.

"Mr. Downs, my mother and I spent a lot of time at the beach." I could tell by her nicely tanned legs. "She wouldn't like all this gloom and doom."

"I understand." I offered.

"I want her buried in her bikini. I'll wear a bikini, too. The pall bearers can be in their swim trunks." She positively glowed.

I was a bit taken aback, but I found my voice and said, "Whatever the family wants."

"Oh thank you, Mr. Downs!" She rose and shook my hand vigorously.

The day of the funeral, Miss Dee, looking like a Barbie doll, showed up in her bikini. Her deceased mom, looking like an older Barbie doll, was also in her bikini. The six, young pall bearers were in their swim trunks, and the minister was a little more subdued in beach attire.

"Mrs. Dee's final reward is going to be a beach in heaven..." the minister began to preach. All through the service Beach Boys music was played, and everyone in the congregation was rocking and rolling with the rhythm of the sounds. Mrs. Dee's headstone had a lady in a bikini carved on it. After the service, family and friends went to the sand dunes at the beach for a beach party. Mom would have approved!

CHEAPER BY THE THREES

One day, a blond woman in her early sixties came in. I found out later this was no dumb blond!

"Mr. Downs? I need to make pre-arrangements for three people."

"Three people?"

"Yes, I care for my husband, my mother, and my step-father, and they are all dying."

My heart went out to this poor woman.

I want to buy three caskets, so I want a big discount."

"A discount?"

"Yes, a discount. It's cheaper to buy in volume. Well, I am."

I couldn't help laughing, and Mrs. Maid got her discount.

MR. BROADSWORTH AND TOILET PAPER

I was standing in the lobby of my funeral home when I saw this Cobra Mustang Convertible drive up. This older lady climbed out who just reeked of wealth. She had to be at least eighty, but was all made up to look years younger.

"I'm here to make arrangements for a funeral." She said curtly.

"Come into my office where we can talk." I offered. After arranging all the necessary items, I always asked a personal item or two for the record.

"What can you tell me about Mr. Broadsworth that I can put into the obituary?" I asked gently.

"He invented toilet paper." She said proudly.

I couldn't help but laugh. "M'am, I thought toilet paper had been around since the Romans."

"No, it hasn't." She insisted. She pulled out old newspaper articles from Vermont to prove her claim.

There it was in black and white. Mr. Broadsworth had invented toilet paper. I always thought toilet paper was here forever, but I was wrong.

ALL IN A DAY'S WORK

ROBERT L. HARRINGTON

I got my insurance license when I retired from the Navy in January, 1975. My company was Paul Revere of Worchester, Massachusetts. For a while, I wore two hats. I was an insurance salesman and a cemetery salesman.

Shortly after being licensed as an insurance salesman, and while still in training, I got a call from a policy holder in Naples. He wanted to talk about final arrangements and cashing one of their policies in to pay for it and to leave the balance to their grandkids.

So, I drove to Naples in my trusty, old '69 Barracuda with no air. The address was on Rum Row which being a Naples neighborhood, sounded exclusive. I was a little intimidated by great wealth, but I went anyway. When I pulled in, I saw two Mercedes in the garage. Why do rich people have to have two of everything? This was even the man's second home. He and his family just came to Florida for the winter. He had a place up North.

When I got out of the car, I looked past the well-manicured lawn and saw a fifty foot yacht in the back canal. I had second thoughts about being there. I walked down to the water's edge, and spoke to the captain who was standing on the deck.

"Good evening."

"Good evening, sir."

"Nice boat."

"Yes, sir. I take good care of it for Mr. Harrington. At the end of the season, I take him and his family back up to Massachusetts. It's a nice trip."

"Sounds like it. Well, I have an appointment with him. Good night."

"Good night, Sir."

Now, I really was getting nervous. I walked back to the main house. This guy's got money out the patoot. "Calm down, Lee." I soothed myself. " He puts his pants on just like everybody else- one leg at a time." I felt better when I knocked on the door.

The maid showed me in and served me cookies and tea while I waited for Mr. Harrington. After about fifteen minutes, a tall, distinguished-looking man appeared. I would guess he was in his early sixties, and although he was casually dressed, he was definitely executive-looking. He extended his hand.

"Good evening. I am Robert L. Harrington." He showed a slight trace of a smile.

"Nice to meet ya. I'm Lee Downs."

His smile grew broader. "I said, I am Robert L. Harrington."

"I know. I'm good with names."

"Don't you recognize my name?"

"It sounds familiar. But I can't place you."

"Look at the cover sheet of one of your sample policies."

Sure enough. There was his signature. Robert L. Harrington, President of the Paul Revere Insurance Company. Suddenly, I became very nervous.

"Let's set up another appointment so I can do some research for you." After a time and date were decided upon, I made my exit, but not before tripping over my own feet and bumping into the tea cart. I could hear Mr. Harrington laughing behind me.

I called my area manager and told him about my experience.

He said, " THE Robert L. Harrington?"

I said, "Of course, THE Robert L. Harrington. Is there another one?"

My manager is in Miami but he flew over to the West Coast, and we went to the appointment with him, together.

It all worked out well. I was salesman of the month with a $7,500 commission check, and the knowledge that Mr. Robert L. Harrington puts his pants on the same way we do- one leg at a time.

HOW TO LOSE A GIRLFRIEND IN ONE EASY STEP

Every year, I loaned a casket to the Matador room to use for their Halloween costume parties. I backed the hearse up to the front door and unloaded the casket, complete with pall bearers, minister, and the whole works. It was a great effect. We got a volunteer to lay in the casket, and I would put a little wedge in the lid, so it wouldn't close. We placed the casket in the front so everyone could pass by and give their condolences. One year, I had a young lady volunteer and she was already nervous.

"I don't know about this, Bob. I'm a little claustrophobic."

"Oh, come on honey. It will be fun." Bob urged. "You already look the part with that black dress and pancake make-up on. Come on, Carol. What do you say?" Bob coaxed sweetly.

"O.K., darling, for you. Besides, it will be fun to hear what people have to say about me after I'm gone." We placed the casket with Carol in it out front, and her friends filed by.

"What a fine girl. She'd give you the shirt off her back." Suzie said.

Mary leaned close to Suzie over the casket. "Well, I heard she was a bit of a lush, myself." Carol laid still and tried not to laugh. The girls were having a good time, so I wondered into the other room for a drink. And then I heard a blood-curdling scream. I dropped my drink and ran back into the front. The lid to the casket was laying on the floor. The casket lid had closed on Carol and in her fright, she found the might to kick the lid off. She was up and out of there in nothing flat, crying and screaming the whole time. Standing to the side was Bob. He had a sheepish grin on his face, and he held the wedge that kept the casket from closing.

"YOU did this!" Carol cried. "The wedding is off!"

"Ah, come on, Carol. We were just having a good time." Explained Bob.

"Well, you can have a good time with someone else. I never want to see you again!" Carol and her girlfriends left and drove away, leaving Bob to ponder his mistake. In the future, I was a little more selective with who I let lay in the casket. I asked Bob if he wanted to do it next year. He didn't answer me. I wonder why.

JUST NAME IT

One of the most interesting sides of being a cemetery owner is the opportunity to design and name Gardens. I was designing a new garden with its main feature being a brick lined pond. I wanted to use it as an urn garden. I couldn't think of a name until one night, while spending the week-end at the beach with my family in our Winnebago camper, I woke up about 3 a.m. with the idea for a name. I dressed and drove to my office to write down my idea before I forgot. The garden was named, "Reflection." It had a reflecting pond and you could reflect on life while there. Yes, the Garden of Reflection.

I also tried to name my gardens to fit the personalities and life styles of the people who would ultimately reside there. In my area of the country, we had a lot of people retiring from up North to play golf in South Florida. They wanted golf clubs as emblems on their markers , so I came up with a Golfer's Garden. It was called, "The Nineteenth Hole" with a feature of a Green with a hole and a flag marked with "19." Other names were "End Zone" and "The Finish Line" for sports enthusiasts. But one of the most unusual things I designed was a Niche Bench out of Georgia Marble where urns could be placed. They were used throughout the cemetery for people to sit on. The benches were sandblasted with the names of the deceased and sealed with the urns inside the legs of the bench. I didn't get much credit for them, but they were big sellers. The only negative comment I got from prospective customers was, "Will people sit on me?"

TOUCH A BOTTLE, TOUCH A BODY

I had a club in Lehigh Acres which is a Veterans club with a little bar in it. One Sunday, this black guy came in. Our regular bar tender was late, so I was tending bar. This guy wanted a beer which I promptly opened and gave to him.

While he was drinking his beer, Clifford, one of our regular customers said, "Hey Lee, tell this guy what you do for a living!"

"I run a cemetery and a crematory."

This guy immediately dropped his drink and said, "YOU TOUCHED MY BOTTLE! YOU TOUCH DEAD BODIES!" He ran out the door.

"I wash my hands, first." I yelled after him, but he was already gone into the night.

The Three Legged Man

Integration may have occurred in the 1960's, but in the deep South, there are still two areas that are still, and probably always will be, segregated: Religion and death. There are black churches and white churches to this day. There are black funeral homes and white funeral homes. In the deep South, in a state like Florida, this will not change. Besides, I think people are more comfortable worshipping with their own ethnic group and burying their dead together.

Now, every black funeral director I've ever met, has been honest and above board except for one. Wilbur Cross wanted to use my cemetery which was more upscale than the city cemetery. He even used some of his own money to buy ten spaces at a time, and he would then in turn sell them to his families. He also had the only black funeral home that would sell cremation services. I had a crematory at my cemetery and he would bring cremation containers to me for cremation with the proper paperwork. At first, we used to joke a lot and be good friends. He came in one day with a cremation container.

"Hey Wilbur," I joked. "If black is beautiful, why does everyone where white to your funerals?"

"I don't know, Lee. If white is right, why does everyone wear black to your funerals?" He had me there.

After we were through joking around, I spot checked his container, and I looked inside and saw a body with three legs.

"Wilbur, this guy can't have three legs. What's the story?"

"It's an amputation. I didn't want to have to pay for two containers and two cremations."

"Wilbur, you know you can't do that." I shook my head. My men separated the leg from the other body and two cremations were done. Needless to say, I checked him from then, on. Wilbur eventually lost his license and funeral home for practices like not burying bodies and spending trust fund money. They found bodies in and around his home. I should have known better the day I looked at the three legged man, but who would have guessed?

ONE SCOOP OR TWO?

Early in my career, I rented an old ice cream store in the worst section of town. It held up to ten bodies. I hadn't built my cooler, yet, and it was easy for the funeral homes around Lee County to leave bodies for me to cremate there because it was centrally located.

I only had one break-in and after they found out what was in there, they stayed away. I could just imagine their reaction.

"Sylvester, you check the cooler. I'll go through the front and the office."

"O.K., Henry. Maybe, I be finding some ice cream to take home to the young-uns. Ha! Ha!" They trash the place looking for cash. Then, Sylvester calls from the cooler.

"Hennnrrrrry!"

"You find something?"

"Yap, and it ain't ice cream!"

"What is it?"

"You better come see." Sylvester's feet were frozen to the floor. Henry makes his way to the cooler.

"Holy mother of God! Let's get out of here!" They make for the door. Sylvester trips on his own feet and falls on the threshold.

"Spooks be following us!" They disappear into the night, never to rob me again.

The LADY of The Evening

One night, I was working late in my office at the cemetery, when I heard a scream that chilled me to the bone. I raced down through the rows of graves, till I saw the source of the screams standing under the street light at the edge of the property.

A young woman in a red mini-skirt, black fishnet stockings, and high heels was standing in front of the last row of graves crying like a baby.

"What's wrong?" I asked, knowing something must be terribly wrong from the way she was dressed.

"Mista," She sobbed. "I don't be hanging around no graveyard. Too many spooks.

"How did you get here?"

"My John- he pushed me oud da de car. He say I was dead tonight, so I might as well be with the dead."

"I'm sorry." How do you console a hooker? I brought her up to the office, gave her some coffee, and called the police. When they picked her up, she was still crying. Oh well, just another average night at the office.

BUMPITY, BUMPITY, PLOP

When I had the little station wagon hearse, I agreed to meet the family at the church with the hearse before the service. On the way from the funeral home to the church a funny thing happened. I had Fred with me in the front seat. Nothing rattles Fred.

Not all the streets in Homosassa were smooth riding at the time. We were going down this one street with a lot of bumps, and I hit this particularly bad bump, and the back door of the station wagon flew open and we heard something sliding. I was shaking in my boots, trying to figure out what to say to the family if anything bad had happened to the casket.

I said, "Fred, get out and see how bad it is."

Fred took a long draw from his pipe, and slowly got out like he was going for a walk in the park.

"Did the casket slide out, Fred?" I asked with fear and trepidation.

"Yup." Fred took another draw of his pipe as he approached my window. "But it didn't hit the ground. It's just kind of hanging there."

"Well, push it back in, you idiot, and shut the door good!" That's the only time I ever lost my cool with Fred. But it rolled off him like water off a duck's back. He got back in the hearse and took another draw on his pipe. Sometimes, I wondered if there wasn't more than tobacco in that pipe, but I knew that wasn't true. It was just Fred's nature. We continued on to the church without the family ever being the wiser.

ROASTING ME

The "All In A Day's Work" section would not be complete without talking about when I was roasted for being, "Boss Of The Year." My old, retired Army buddy, Tony Casella, was always picking on me because I was Navy.

When it was his turn to roast me, he asked, "Has anyone ever wondered why Lee always wears the same jacket but has dozens of different trousers?"

There was no response from the crowd.

"That's because only the top half of the casket is open, and you only see one jacket."

"Are you calling me a deadbeat?" I yelled back.

"Yes." Tony answered, and the crowd erupted in laughter.

EPILOGUE

I have really enjoyed recalling and reliving these stories, and I hope you have enjoyed reading them. While there is a kernel of truth in each and every story, my ghost writer, Kathleen has a wild imagination and turned some of these anecdotes into short stories.

If you recognize a person in these stories as yourself or someone you know, it may be coincidental or it may be you. I'll never tell. Either way, you will see these stories are factual and fanciful at the same time. This book represents the interesting and sometimes, funny sides to our serious times with death and life.

Most of the names have been changed for obvious reasons. Some are actual names, as these people asked me to use their real names. But whether the names are real or made up, there are some of us in all these characters. That is why we find it funny. Remember, if you don't laugh at life and death, you end up crying. I'd rather laugh, myself. Thanks for the memories.

R.I.P.

HERE LIES LEE DOWNS,
HE ALWAYS WAS A CLOWN
HE'S NOT DAFT,
HE JUST MADE YOU LAUGH
SO WIPE THAT TEAR FROM YOUR EYE,
IT'S NOT SO BAD TO DIE- LAUGHING

UNITED STATES OF FLORIDA

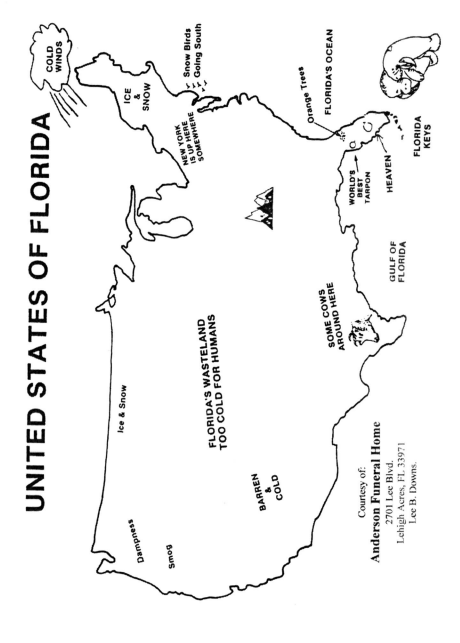

COLD WINDS

ICE & SNOW

Snow Birds Going South

NEW YORK IS UP HERE SOMEWHERE

Orange Trees

FLORIDA'S OCEAN

WORLD'S BEST TARPON

HEAVEN

FLORIDA KEYS

GULF OF FLORIDA

SOME COWS AROUND HERE

FLORIDA'S WASTELAND TOO COLD FOR HUMANS

Ice & Snow

BARREN & COLD

Dampness

Smog

Courtesy of:
Anderson Funeral Home
2701 Lee Blvd.
Lehigh Acres, FL 33971
Lee B. Downs.

128

UNITED STATED OF FLORIDA

Our Funeral Home was in S.W. Florida and a lot of our families were from up north, we affectionately call them Snow Birds, when I ask them where they were from they would reply New York or Chicago or Cleveland or elsewhere. I would say Oh, I've heard of that its up near Jacksonville . So they wouldn't think I was a country bumpkin and didn't know my geography, I invented the United States of Florida. The families loved it and would always take one home.

CPSIA information can be obtained
at www.ICGtesting.com
Printed in the USA
FSOW01n1047050416
18843FS

9 781438 902319